BLOOD DAZZLER

Blood Dazzler

POEMS

PATRICIA SMITH

COFFEE HOUSE PRESS
Minneapolis

COFFEE HOUSE PRESS books are available to the trade through our primary distributor, Consortium Book Sales & Distribution, www.cbsd.com or (800) 283-3572. For personal orders, catalogs, or other information, write to: info@coffeehousepress.org.

Coffee House Press is a nonprofit literary publishing house. Support from private foundations, corporate giving programs, government programs, and generous individuals helps make the publication of our books possible. We gratefully acknowledge their support in detail in the back of this book. To you and our many readers around the world, we send our thanks for your continuing support.

LIBRARY OF CONGRESS CIP INFORMATION

Smith, Patricia, 1955–
Blood dazzler : poems / by Patricia Smith.
p. cm.
ISBN 978-1-56689-218-6 (alk. paper)
1. Hurricane Katrina, 2005—Poetry. 2. New Orleans (La.)—Poetry. I. Title.
PS3569.M537839B56 2008
811'.54—DC22

ACKNOWLEDGMENTS

Grateful acknowledgement to the editors of the following magazines and anthologies, in which these poems first appeared: *Chautauqua Literary Journal,* "34"; *Callaloo,* "Ethel's Sestina"; *Sou'wester,* "Voodoo Authentica"; *The November 3rd Club,* "What to Tweak"; *Split This Rock/Beloit Poetry Journal,* "She Sees What It Sees" and "The President Flies Over"; *America: What's My Name?* (Wind Publications, 2007): "Michael Brown," "Loot" and "What Was the First Sound."

And thanks to Dennis Nurkse, Charles Martin, Tim Seibles and the inimitable Annie Finch, my mentors in the Stonecoast MFA program, who nurtured and strengthened "Dazzler"; Carl Phillips and Cyrus Cassells, whose comments were invaluable; the entire Cave Canem community; and Urban Bush Women choreographer/dancer Paloma McGregor, who blessed these words with heat and motion.

Every word is for my granddaughter Mikaila
and my husband Bruce,
who taught me all I know about love.

And for the people of the Gulf Coast,
who redefined faith.

PROLOGUE—
AND THEN SHE OWNS YOU

This is not morning. There is a nastiness
slowing your shoes, something you shouldn't step in.
It's shattered beads, stomped flowers, vomit—
such stupid beauty,

beauty you can stick a manicured finger
into and through, beauty that doesn't rely
on any sentence the sun chants, it's whiskey
swelter blown scarlet.

Call this something else. Last night it had a name,
a name wedged between an organ's teeth, a name
pumping a virgin unawares, a curse word.
Wail it, regardless,

Weak light, bleakly triumphant, will unveil scabs,
snippets of filth music, cars on collapsed veins.
The whole of gray doubt slithers on solemn skin.
Call her New Orleans.

Each day she wavers, not knowing how long she
can stomach the introduction of needles,
the brash, boozed warbling of bums with neon crowns,
necklaces raining.

She tries on her voice, which sounds like cigarettes,
pubic sweat, brown spittle lining a sax bell
the broken heel on a drag queen's scarlet slings.
Your kind of singing.

Weirdly in love, you rhumba her edges, drink
fuming concoctions, lick your lukewarm breakfast
directly from her crust. Go on, admit it.
You are addicted

to her brick hips, the thick swerve she elicits,
the way she kisses you, her lies wide open.
She prefers alleys, crevices, basement floors.
Hell, let her woo you.

This kind of romance dims the worth of soldiers,
bends and breaks the back, sips manna from muscle,
tells you *Leave your life.* Pack your little suitcase,
flee what is rigid

and duly prescribed. Let her touch that raw space
between cock and calm, the place that scripts such jazz.
Let her pen letters addressed to your asking.
You s-s-stutter.

New Orleans's, p-please. Don't. Blue is the color
stunning your tongue. At least the city pretends
to remember to be listening.
She grins with glint tooth,

wiping your mind blind of the wife, the children.
the numb ritual of job and garden plot.
Gently, she leads you out into the darkness
and makes you drink rain.

BLOOD DAZZLER

CONTENTS

5 P.M., TUESDAY, AUGUST 23, 2005

"Data from an Air Force reserve unit reconnaissance aircraft . . . along with observations from the Bahamas and nearby ships . . . indicate the broad low pressure area over the southeastern Bahamas has become organized enough to be classified as tropical depression twelve."
—NATIONAL HURRICANE CENTER

A muted thread of gray light, hovering ocean,
becomes throat, pulls in wriggle, anemone, kelp,
widens with the want of it. I become
a mouth, thrashing hair, an overdone eye. How dare
the water belittle my thirst, treat me as just
another
small
disturbance,

try to feed me
from the bottom of its hand?

I will require praise,
unbridled winds to define my body,
a crime behind my teeth
because

every woman begins as weather,
sips slow thunder, knows her hips. Every woman
harbors a chaos, can

wait for it, straddling a fever.

For now,
I console myself with small furies,
those dips in my dawning system. I pull in
a bored breath. The brine shivers.

11 A.M., WEDNESDAY, AUGUST 24, 2005

"Satellite imagery . . . Doppler radar data from the Bahamas and Miami . . . indicate [tropical depression twelve] has become much better organized . . . has strengthened into tropical storm Katrina."
—NATIONAL HURRICANE CENTER

The difference in a given name. What the calling,
the hard K, does to the steel of me,
how suddenly and surely it grants me
pulse, petulance. Now I can do

my own choking. I can thread my fingers
with grimace and spit

zephyr, a gentle marking
of the very first time I felt

that crisp, bladed noun
in my own mouth.

5 P.M., THURSDAY, AUGUST 25, 2005

The National Hurricane Center upgrades tropical storm Katrina
to Hurricane Katrina.

My eye takes in so much—
what it craves, what I never hoped to see.
It doesn't care about pain, is eons away
from the ego's thump, doesn't hesitate
to scan the stark, adjust for distance,
unravel the world for no reason at all, except that it

hungers.

It needs to croon in every screeching hue,
strives to know waltz, hesitation,
small changes in sun. It spots
weeping, then wants to see its sound. It spies
pattern and restlessly hunts the solid drum.

The eye

pushes my rumbling bulk forward,
urges me to see
what it sees.

4

7 P.M., THURSDAY, AUGUST 25, 2005

Hurricane Katrina makes landfall in Florida.

I see

         what this language does

and taste

         soil on my tongue

and feel

         brick splintering spine

and hear

         them

and want it

         all

WHY NEW ORLEANS IS

Rollicking karaoke sweats the walls of a red-washed room,
and six southern Illinois breasts swag in unison
to "You Can't Hurry Love." These A-line skirted divas
want that *so* not to be true, the way they click
hard Pilated hips in time to a layered Negro beat,
drawing lustful licks from the boys at the bar.

This is why New Orleans is—
to scrub and soil us in parallel,
to serve up patented alibis for pluck and perfume,
then peel us down to silly shimmying warblers
on a sloped stage slick with beer and Tabasco.
This is why we stumble into stinging neon showers
of beads, feathers, and voodoo figurines—
because we need to hurt in public,
throw up a little in a ghosted alley,
close pert mouths around the cocks of strangers.

Every damned body needs a midnight stage,
an intricate accordioned theme song,
a little country that worships at our dime-store altar.
We can rearrange our bruised religions
while pouting over pristine snack packs
on jumbo jets hurtling home.
Hungering for just a little harbored nasty,
we realize that each breath is strangely bladed,
and we hiss it, then: *Love, c'mon, dammit, hurry up.*

MAN ON THE TV SAY

Go. He say it simple, gray eyes straight on and watered,
he say it in that machine throat they got.
On the wall behind him, there's a moving picture
of the sky dripping something worse than rain.
Go, he say. Pick up y'all black asses and run.
Leave your house with its splinters and pocked roof,
leave the pork chops drifting in grease and onion,
leave the whining dog, your one good watch,
that purple church hat, the mirrors.
Go. Uh-huh. Like our bodies got wheels and gas,
like at the end of that running there's an open door
with dry and song inside. He act like we supposed
to wrap ourselves in picture frames, shadow boxes,
and bathroom rugs, then walk the freeway, racing
the water. *Get on out.* Can't he see that our bodies
are just our bodies, tied to what we know?
Go. So we'll go. Cause the man say it strong now,
mad like God pointing the way outta Paradise.
Even he got to know our favorite ritual is root,
and that none of us done ever known a horizon,
especially one that cools our dumb running,
whispering urge and constant: *This way. Over here.*

ONLY EVERYTHING I OWN

This is my house.
This was my grandfather's house.
This is my thin wood, spidered pane.
These are my cobwebs, my four walls,
my silverfish, my bold roaches.
I bury my hands in that little garden,
cool them in the broken earth.
My food comes from my garden.
At my table, I slice the peppers,
seed the tomatoes, chop mint,
rip bitter green into wooden bowls.
The tiny pine table is my whole kitchen,
daddy's legacy, my certain warm nurture.
I dream loud in this house. I pull my bed
down from that wall, and I fall to my knees
next to it to question this shelter.
I sleep while a limp breeze dies at the window,
waking to dawn tangled with my dust.
This is my house.

Let's step out into the steam,
sip new breath from a Mason jar,
find a sleeping rhythm for our chairs.
Let's wait patiently for the rain.
That blistered sky has learned my days
and hates me for everything I have. As it should.

VOODOO I: LOVE AND PASSION

Offered by Voodoo Authentica Cultural Center & Collection, New Orleans: "Packaged in Parchment envelope with our logo wax seal . . . Our Authentic Voodoo Magic Spells & Formulas are available for the following magickal purposes . . . "

Sudden a battered bongo in her layback,
hair root lazed sizzle, fluent spine of silver,
heart a hall of solo mirror, stuttered,
and why is everything swollen?
Her breasts walloping,
his cock a thrilling cerulean,
damned adjectives all over everything.
The heart relishes its role as machine,
knowing no one but God can numb the forward
and meanwhile, it's fuck, fuck, fuck,
unbooked thrums just because.
An appetite rhythmed like this must boast booms,
and the mirror can't take it. Eventually,
a shard escapes.
Something bleeds.

WON'T BE BUT A MINUTE

Tie Luther B to that cypress. He gon' be all right.
That dog done been rained on before,
he done been here a day or two by hisself before,
and we sho' can't take him. Just leave him
some of that Alpo and plenty of water.
Bowls and bowls of water.
We gon' be back home soon this thing pass over.
Luther B gon' watch the place while we gone.
You heard the man—he said *Go*—and you know
white folks don't warn us 'bout nothing unless
they scared too. We gon' just wait this storm out.
Then we come on back home. Get our dog.

8 A.M., SUNDAY, AUGUST 28, 2005

Katrina becomes a Category 5 storm, the highest possible rating.

For days, I've been offered blunt slivers
of larger promises—even flesh,
my sweet recurring dream,
has been tantalizingly dangled before me.
I have crammed my mouth with buildings,
brushed aside skimpy altars,
snapped shut windows to bright shatter
with my fingers. And I've warned them, soft:
You must not know my name.

Could there be other weather,
other divas stalking the cringing country
with insistent eye?
Could there be other rain,
laced with the slick flick of electric
and my own pissed boom? Or could this be

it, finally,
my praise day,
all my fists at once?

Now officially a bitch, I'm confounded by words—
all I've ever been is starving, fluid, and noise.
So I huff a huge sulk, thrust out my chest,
open wide my solo swallowing eye.

You must not know

Scarlet glare fixed on the trembling crescent,

I fly.

INCONVENIENT

Go.
What, again? What nuisance, this back and forth.
But even the blessed must bow to damp tantrums.
Some network blathering, ominous graphics,
and we pack the steamer with overnight,
lash the boat to its mooring, wrap the new guest house
up like some stern little package. And for what?
So some dreary witch with a name bigger than she's worth
can drip scare into nightfall, turn one day, maybe two,
into missed manicures, grayish harping, dull dinners
of canned soup. *Go.* And this time, again, it's serious.
What it is is just more windy yelping by wild-eyed anchors,
round-the-clock warnings followed by wet drumming
in the flower beds, stretched nerves, maybe a hint of mold.
At least twice a year, we deal with the plumped drama
of an oversold storm, watching as the sky bulges,
leaks melodrama, postpones our garden parties.

Best to consider this whole mess a holiday,
a simple trade, one home for its vacation version.
Best to cram our luggage into the idling Lincoln
and wait while my husband revels in busywork,
clawing through his toolbox, hammering a thumbnail
and strengthening every room's surface with tape.
After he slides his pampered girth behind the wheel,
we point the car toward rumored sun, scan the sky
for signs. Again, we run. Left to me, I wouldn't budge.
Up here the dollar sings. We pay for this boredom.

COMPANY'S COMING

Hell, I rode the back of the last one.
It was all they said it was, but I rode her good.
The key to making it through
is to strap yourself hard against a thing,
keep your mouth shut tight
lest all that wrong weather gets in.
She gon' slap the black offa you now,
don't get me wrong, but that big fuss
don't last but a hot minute.
Just lay yourself flat while ol' girl
points her chaos toward your upturned ass,
just hold onto maybe while she blows away
what you thought would hold you down.
Ain't no feeling like the one when it's all over
and you still here. So go on, peek through the blinds.
See a mad-ass woman with us in her eye?
She picks her teeth with prayers. Get ready to ride.

THE DAWN OF LUTHER B'S BEST DAY

Luther B, months mangy and chained down
against m'dear's shade tree, feels a little thrill
shoot through his planted paws, sniffs questions
in the swirled air. Suddenly the day is touching him.
The mutt whimpers, raps yaps, twists his stout squatness,
strains against thick links, moans a wavering O.

But nobody's coming this time, nobody to scratch
the dead skin behind his ear, no m'dear hobbling out
in scuffs and shift, cussing, carrying a fresh can a' heaven.

All that's reachin' for him now is the sky, the God daddy,
pressing down fast, cracks of purple in its fingers.
Luther B writhes on his back in the dirt, tumbling the fleas,
then forces himself still. Snout upturned, he watches
his deliverance come closer. With the first plops of rain,
he snarls low and realizes just what kinda dog he is—
itchy, utterly bitchless, locked to the skin of a tree,
but fat with future. And now a cool day comin'. Hot damn.

GHAZAL

There were early indications that this was no mere rain
when the B-boys stopped their ballin' to shout *Yo! You hear rain?*

But air just danced wrong around them. Doomed brick and wood shivered
a little. Children saw no reason not to go near rain—

storms had roared through their little lives, cleansing and slamming shut
whole seasons, putting on a lushness show. Should they fear rain?

Never. They tilted faces up, giggled and swooned beneath
the battering wet, felt denims slog with weight, with sheer rain.

To punctuate their flailing dance, gusts swirled and grew heavy
with stone. Sparks slapped tree sides, chaos roared its loud and clear reign.

Everyone else tried hard to vanish the sight of dripping
nomads rowing cardboard boxes. No, this was not mere rain.

Knowing it wouldn't end, mothers pulled whole lives to rooftops
and wailed for light, wept a blue note we won't know. A tear? Rain?

Still they are there, gasping for new sky, while the B-boys search
the soggy wreckage for game. They curse the disappeared rain.

10:30 A.M., SUNDAY, AUGUST 28, 2005

Their hard-pressed hair is topped with every manner
of church hat—ski-sloped satin, velvet, or brocade crowns
adorned with glittered netting, babbling florals,
even stunned fake bluebirds. The senior choir
warms up, humming tumult away from their joints.
Caged in impossibly proper brown serge, the elders
amble to their front pews and gaze upon the preacher
with unquestioned reverence. They try not to notice how small
he really is, cause he's the only one there who knows Jesus
by His first name. Rev's an itty bitty somethin', though.
If they all took a deep breath and let it out in his direction,
they could lift him off his feet. They could pray for themselves.

SHE SEES WHAT IT SEES

The eye of Hurricane Katrina passes over New Orleans.

And the levees crackled,
and baptism rushed through the ward,
blasting the boasts from storefronts,
sweeping away the rooted, the untethered,
bending doors, withering the strength of stoops.
Damn!, like a mantra, drummed and constant comment
on the rising drink. *Shit!* Skirts shamelessly hefted,
pants legs ripped away, babies balanced in the air.
But still, acceptance, flurries of *ha ha I'll be damned,*
because breakage has always been backdrop
and water—well, water sears through them,
drenches their white garb and reveals a savior's face.
It has provided hard passage,
sparkled its trickery
and shepherded them
to death before.

WHAT WAS THE FIRST SOUND

it made, heaven's seam splitting?
Was the sound purple?

The sound was purple,
throbbing like a new-torn wound
under August drape.

Under August drape,
Miss Katrina's swollen gaze
considered bodies.

Consider bodies,
already filled with water
but secure in bone.

Secure in its bone,
a squat building shit bricks.
The sound was purple.

The sound was purple.
And only mutts, priestesses,
and tree trunks heard it.

Tree trunks heard it
ripping spit through matted leaves.
Wind found its color.

Wind found its color
and cast an eerie alto
to the first plops of rain

To the first plops of rain,
add the sound of purple,
shitted bricks losing bone,
the seam splitting and finally spilling

bodies

already filled with water.

LUTHER B RIDES OUT THE STORM

Lord ham mercy, m'dear moaned,
slow and real Baptist like, every time some kink
swerved her day—an August noon sweatin'
the sugar out of her just-pressed hair,
a run in her last pair of church stockings.
Luther B sympathized with a cock of his thick head.
Now, in the looped reloop of dog thought,
he wonders about that Lord, and mercy,
and m'dear's little surrenders, surrenders.

His wet yelps and winding croon reach nothing.
Wobbling, he latches muzzle to the wall of wind.
There's got to be some good livin' at the end of this,
maybe a pork chop with some religion still hangin' from it,
or a skillet scrape of m'dear's fat oxtails and onion rice.
Bet there's daybreaks stackin' up behind those clouds,
regular, with quiet moons behind, all rowed up, ready.

The day's pewter howling wounds a rib,
darkens Luther B's itching with blood.

Paddling in frantic blue circle,
he fights his slippery chain,
treads toward a little bit more of remember—
Damn dog ain't nuthin' but trouble.
But I loves me some Luther B.
I loves him to death.

GETTIN' HIS TWANG ON

George Bush plays guitar with country singer Mark Willis;
2 p.m., August 30, 2005

The President strums the vessel's flat face,
his stance ossifying, his dead eyes fixed
on the numb, escaping chord. Everyone

feigns amazement at the tuneless thrumming.
They spur him on with spurious laughter.
The cowboy grins through the terrible din,

the flashing bulbs, the rampant ass kissing.
And in the Ninth, a choking woman wails
Look like this country done left us for dead.

That's our soundtrack, and here comes the chorus.
The lyrics, siphoned of light, are shadow
in everyone's throat. He plucks strings. We sing.

UP ON THE ROOF

Up on the roof, stumbling slickstep, you wave all your sheets and your blouses,
towels, bandannas, and denims, and etch what you ask on the morning:

When are they coming to save us? cause sinking is all that you're feeling.
Blades spin so close to your breathing. Their noise, crazy roar, eats invective,

blotting out words as you scream them. They turn your beseeching to vapor.
Water the dark hue of anger now laps at the feet you can't stand on.

Cameras obsess with your chaos. Now think how America sees you:
Gold in your molars and earlobes. Your naps knotted, craving a brushing.

You clutch your babies regardless, keep roaring your spite to where God is.
Breast pushes hard past your buttons. Then mud cracks its script on your forearm,

each word a misspelled agenda. But here come the flyboys to save you,
baskets to cram your new life in, the drama of fetching and swinging.

Some people think that you're crazy. As you descend from the heavens,
you choose to head for the questions. The earth and its water. The swallow.

VOODOO II: MONEY

If magick brings it, it will be tainted, damp, ill-hued,
the wrong patriot will grimace from its center,
denominations will mean nothing. Money that passes
through hands blackened with the powder of ill wish,
hands spiced with incantation oils,
won't ever spend well. It will appear green and viable
only for a second, a second just wide enough
to turn you into a certified fool—then, as you hold
it in front of you like a shield against weather,
you will know. It's too thin to hold tomorrow back.

WHAT TO TWEAK

Italicized excerpts are from an Aug. 31, 2005 e-mail from Marty Bahamonde to his boss Michael Brown, head of the Federal Emergency Management Agency. Bahamonde was one of the only FEMA employees in New Orleans at the time.

Aug. 31, 12:20 p.m. Re: New Orleans

Sir, I know that you know the situation is past critical. Here are some things you might not know.

> Rainbows warp when you curse them.
> I have held a shiver of black child against my body.
> The word *river* doesn't know edges.
> God wouldn't do this.
> There's a Chevy growing in that tree.
> Here, I am so starkly white.
> Sometimes bullets make perfect sense.
> Eventually the concrete will buckle.
> They won't stop screeching at me.
> I have passed out all my gum.
> So many people are thirsty.
> A kid breathes wet against my thigh.
> He calls me father.

Hotels are kicking people out . . . .

> No one is prepared for their sulking shadows.
> They sully sleek halls, leave smudges on grand glass.

They double negative, sport clothes limp with ache.
These people don't know this place,
this costly harbor where they have always pointed,
eyes bucked and overwhelmed,
giddy with the conjure of mirrored silver
and whole cups dedicated to tea.
In the sudden midst of glorious this,
they fill their cavernous pockets with faith.
Why didn't we bolt the doors
before they began to dream?

thousands gathering in the streets with no food or water . . .

The weakened mob veers into the open for breath.
Ashy babies bellow, B-boys hurl gold-toothed *fuck-its,*
everyone asks for food. And the heat singes art
on bare backs, sucks tears from parched skin.
It's true there is no food, but water is everywhere.
The demon has chapped their rusty ankles,
reddened the throats of babies, smashed homes to mist.
It is water that beats down without taking a breath
and points its dank mossy finger at their faith.
I have killed you, it patters.
I have bled you dry.

Hundreds still being rescued from homes.

Or not.
Death has an insistent iron smell, oversweet rot
loud enough to wither certain woods.
Behind sagging doors specters swirl,
grow huge-limbed, stink brilliance.
And up on the roofs of tombs,
sinking mothers claw the sky,

pray the rising river away from their scream.
The moon refuses to illuminate their overtures,
winking dim then winking shut.
From the papery peaks of three-flats,
shots and weeping in the starless dark.
If you listen, you can hear the dying.
It creaks odd and high,
a song slowly larger than the singer.

*Evacuation in process. Plans developing for dome evacuation but
hotel situation adding to problem. We are out of food and running out
of water at the dome. Plans in works to address the critical need.*

Stifle the stinking, shut down the cameras,
wave Dubya down from the sky.
Subtract the babies, unarm the flailers,
Hose that wailing bitch down!
Draw up a blueprint, consider detention,
throw them some cash from a bag.
Tell them it's God, ply them with preachers,
padlock the rest of the map.
Hand them a voucher, fly in some Colonel,
twist the volume knob hard.
Turn down the TV, distract them with vision,
pull out your hammer and nail.
Sponge off their shoulders, suckle their children,
prop them upright for the lens.
Tolerate ranting, dazzle with card tricks,
pin flags on absent lapels.
Try not to breathe them, fan them with cardboard,
say that their houses will rise.
Play them some music, swear you hear engines,
drape their stooped bodies with beads.
Salute their resilience, tempt them with future,

surrender your shoes to the mud.
Promise them trailers, pass out complaint forms,
draft a law wearing their names.
Say help is coming, say help is coming,
then say that help's running late.
Shrink from their clutches, lie to their faces,
explain how the levies grew thin.
Mop up the vomit, cringe at their crudeness,
audition their daughters for rape.
Stomp on their sleeping, outrun the gangsters,
pass out American flags.

*DMAT staff working in deplorable conditions. The sooner we can get
the medical patients out, the sooner we can get them out.*

Breathing bladed, blood tinged black,
their stark diseases mystify, ooze unbridled.
Heat stuns their grip on history,
so they keep attempting to walk back
into remembered days of weather
that never grew more difficult than rain.
They crave the reign of simple delta,
when skinned pig, peppered collards,
and a bottle of red heat signaled a day gone right.
So they keep trying to walk, to force their feet
into the now-obscenity of a straight line,
to begin with that first blessing—*forward, forward,*
not getting the joke of their paper shoes,
not knowing the sidewalks are gone.

Brown:

Thanks for update. Anything specific I need to do

or tweak?

MICHAEL BROWN

I am not much
beyond buttoned cuff,
blade-scraped cheek,
hair glued flat with tap water, then oiled
for cool precision. There is always veneer
to be had, a greasy English to be borrowed.

All men should be instructed
to run past mirrors,
our eyes should never reach for us,
should never create image to be answered.

I am a man, a stacker of clean paper.
Tiny storms inhale my hours.

M'DEAR THINKS ON LUTHER B

Bet he done broke loose. Rottweiler,
bull, whatever that dog is, he can eat
and he can swim. And show them teeth
like that's supposed to scare somebody.
Luther B, much as that dog like living,
he know what to do with some water.
Knowing him, he probably backstrokin',
swimmin' the Ninth, looking for something
good to fill that big greedy gut of his.
Thinkin' this all a show put on just for him.
Nah, don't y'all worry none 'bout Luther B.
He harder to shake than a bucktoothed man.

KATRINA

I was birthed restless and elsewhere

gut dragging and bulging with ball lightning, slush,
broke through with branches, steel

I was bitch-monikered, hipped, I hefted
a whip rain, a swirling sheet of grit.

Scraping toward the first of you, hungering for wood, walls,
unturned skin. With shifting and frantic mouth, I loudly loved
the slow bones

of elders, fools, and willows.

VOODOO III:
GAMBLING AND LUCKY LOTTO

Certain numbers for unlucky Tuesdays,
others for dreams of droop-eyed felines,
multiples of three for scorched black beans,
screen doors, visitors after midnight.

Today, though, everybody's playing *rain.*
The digit combos suggest warped wood,
brick dust, wind tunnels, devilment.
Numbers say *mud* and *hurricane,*
but *drowning* most of all.

DON'T DRINK THE WATER

A dog's sudden slickness slices such raw terror
through the surface, its collar biting into bloat,
jaunty bone-shaped tag a dollop of odd on black.

Sluggish miracle silvers of oil clutch Tuesday's
stupid brazen light and wink gorgeous while belching
sudden scattered flames. And over there, a window—

its dusty shadowed pane spidered into hundreds
of crusted pins in search of bared skin or dwelling.
Skimming leviathan vermin, their teeth bared, snort

the sugar of such leaving. Gleeful, they survive
on odor, exploded food, the gooey glued spine
of—wait—that looks like *How Stella Got Her Groove Back*.

Some mama's body, gaseous, a dimming star splayed
and so gently spinning, threatens its own soft seams,
collides sloppily with mattresses, power lines,

shards of four-doors. And trees, of course, are the monsters
we always knew they were. With lengthy gnarled arms raw
and lightning-slashed, they fist through the dark rushing depths

to etch hungered talons against blue. On the soft
bark of an oak, *H-E-L-p*, knifed in fever.
The water's black teeth reach for the helpless vowel.

Networks deftly edit and craft this sexy glint
of sudden ocean, wait for mama's bobbing bulk
to sweetly swirl into view, framed—*now!*—by the word.

Beneath this wet, at deeper wet, soulless shit reigns,
a sludge of skitters and screams, everything that drains
from the dying curdles, folds into hellish soup.

Winn-Dixie checkers, baby daddies, vague Baptists,
scared cops slog through, the slow wilting jazz of their legs
razored by the murk. What claws at their stride is piss,

lies about wind. What slows their forward is fetid,
fervently lapping, E coli, fuel, old meat.
Nudges toward hellfire hiss against forearm and knee.

It's almost laughable, this wading through the thick
toward other rain. That mama whirls such splayed grace
on drenched sky. Better to rest, succumb to float, shine.

LOOT

Exploded marts, ripped wide aloose,
bleed unchecked Negroes
who crumple under gaudy electrics,
balance towers of stiff white Jordans,
push squeaky shopping carts
crammed to spilling. Giddy shoppers
circle and howl, bellowing their felonies.
They groan under bassinets and vacuums,
balance Magnavox across blazing shoulders,
hurtle for their drowned addresses.

Soggy boxes, weighted with juice bottles,
baby formula, and squat jars of pasta sauce,
lose their bottoms in the current and—*shit!*—
that sudden splintered treasure
bloodies ankles and sparkles the boulevard,
stubbornly lighting the way.

THE PRESIDENT FLIES OVER

Aloft between heaven and them,

I babble the landscape—what staunch, vicious trees,
what cluttered roads, slow cars. This is my

country as it was gifted me—victimless, vast.
The soundtrack buzzing the air around my ears
continually loops ditties of eagles and oil.
I can't choose. Every moment I'm awake,
aroused instrumentals channel theme songs,
speaking
what I cannot.

I don't ever have to come down.
I can stay hooked to heaven,
dictating this blandness.
My flyboys memorize flip and soar.
They'll never swoop real enough
to resurrect that other country,

won't ever get close enough to give name
to tonight's dreams darkening the water.

I understand that somewhere it has rained.

VOODOO IV:
POWER AND DOMINATION

How many times do we stop during the day
to tally the things we control?
We boldly eye those we presume
to be weaker, pitying their wince and scrounge,
their boxy little residences,
the multitudes who lie about loving them.
It's strange how badly we need a bottom,
a meandering dirt road to trek and curse.
An envelope rubbed with sage will give you
a whip of words. You will become a monster,
and their small selves will be swallowed.

TANKAS

Never has there been
a wind like this. Its throaty
howl has memorized
my name. And it calls, and it
calls, and lamb to ax, I come.

I have three children,
but only two arms. He falls
and barely splashes,
that's how incredibly light
he is—was. How death whispers.

I lie on my back
on this roof, dazed by the stars
blazing on pure black.
I croon feverish, off-key
to drown out the water's teeth.

I found my sister
whirling in the peppered blue,
my father under rock,
and then myself, fingering
the hard barrel of a gun.

The breath just before
the last breath harbors the soul
encased in a verb.
I know the word by heart now.
Oh, I wish I could tell you.

Here is what drowning
feels like—God's hands smothering
your heart. And the thumps
grow slower, slower, until
He takes back your name. Lifts you.

Balanced on my toes,
foul panties drooped to ankles,
I scan the street, then
squeeze both of my dead eyes shut,
teeter, shit on the sidewalk.

Go, they said. Go. Go.
Get out before the rain comes,
before you can't run,
before the mud smells your skin
and begins its swirl, its hug.

What's in the water?
What nips me, sucks at my legs,
bumps and leaves bruises?
I will walk, but I won't look
at the flow that says *Stop. Rest.*

I see how the men
look at my bended body,
like its first rapist
was rain. And now they hover,
because I have been broken.

Can't find my rhythm,
can't pinpoint that fleeting pulse.
The drum at my core
taps stubborn single lyric,
then rimshot. I cross over.

SUPERDOME

I did not demand they wade through the overflow from toilets,
chew their own nails bloody in place of a meal.

I didn't feed their squalling babies chewing gum,
force them to pee out loud in gutters,
or make them lick their own sweat for healing salt.

I pity the women who had to sleep with their legs
slammed shut, and the elders with their rheumy eyes
trained on my crown even after it was ripped away.

Glittering and monstrous, I was defined by a man's hand,
my tight musculature coiled beneath plaster and glass.
I was never their church, although I disguised myself as shelter
and relentlessly tested their faith.

DREAM LOVER

"We had babies in there. Little babies getting raped."
—NEW ORLEANS POLICE CHIEF EDDIE COMPASS ON OPRAH
WINFREY'S SHOW, SEPT. 6, 2005

"We don't have any substantiated rapes."
—NEW ORLEANS POLICE CHIEF EDDIE COMPASS, SEPT. 5, 2005

Add
sleepy oblivious children to
waterlogged thugs to
overstretched mothers finally dozing
and surely you must expect exceptions
to any rule, you must know that grasping
for life means subtle, supple, new, that some moment
inside our chests snaps inane and even a tiny heat
feeds a hollow.
This is difference,
the abandoning of usual,
this is specific fever. I have no shirt
that recalls my muscle, no meat or milk,
no bed that is mine,
but I will have this bumbler, this exquisite child,
this fresh refugee who will teach me the runaway drum
of the body. I will peel away shields and have this. I will
praise circumstance and have this. Because this
is not a day as days have been.
* * *

At its dripped borders, I am raven and cocked,
baptized in standing water,
insatiable, inked specter.
As you desired, I have fucked them all,
left them reversed and victim.
My romances scamper the bleachers, scrambling
to cover their skin. Craving absolution,
they search the faces of strangers.
Never really expecting an answer, they ask each one,
Do you know my name?

VOODOO V: ENEMY BE GONE

The storm left a wound seeping,
a boulevard yawning, some
memories fractured, a
kiss exploded, she left
no stone resting, a bone
army floating, rats sated,
she left the horizon sliced
and ornery, she left in a hurry,
in a huff, in all her glory,
she took with her a kingdom
of sax and dream books,
a hundred scattered chants,
some earth burned in her
name, and she took flight,
all pissed and raucous, like
a world-hipped woman
makin' room.

MS. THANG SLOSHES IN
THE DIRECTION OF HOME

This damned trod spells ruin for her party pumps.
She slogs through in fuchsia suede, fiercely arrowed,
and the going is torturous. Her beauty
has never known this mud, this stupid slither
clogging her path. One stiletto collapses.
and she rips them both off, cringes at the feel
of her pampered feet on this shifting, shifting.
She thought that being a woman meant filling
the body with rain, reveling in the sweet rounding.
But now she is bent, whisper bearded.
The carefully stifled cock escapes, swings loose
beneath her snug skirt. And suddenly the boy
in her is huge, slowing the brazen sashay.
Old muscles swell, beg her to dive and push
like a man, master the water, swim
like a bitch with an Olympic agenda.
But she prefers the brave dramatic hobble
of the damaged dive, the occasional
muddied stun, the ways hips suggest progression.
Oh yeah, it's the biggest stage she's ever seen.
She must work it. There's a limelight somewhere.

ETHEL'S SESTINA

Ethel Freeman's body sat for days in her wheelchair outside the New Orleans Convention Center. Her son Herbert, who had assured his mother that help was on the way, was forced to leave her there once she died.

Gon' be obedient in this here chair,
gon' bide my time, fanning against this sun.
I ask my boy, and all he says is *Wait.*
He wipes my brow with steam, says I should sleep.
I trust his every word. Herbert my son.
I believe him when he says help gon' come.

Been so long since all these suffrin' folks come
to this place. Now on the ground 'round my chair,
they sweat in my shade, keep asking my son
could that be a bus they see. It's the sun
foolin' them, shining much too loud for sleep,
making us hear engines, wheels. Not yet. Wait.

Lawd, some folks prayin' for rain while they wait,
forgetting what rain can do. When it come,
it smashes living flat, wakes you from sleep,
eats streets, washes you clean out of the chair
you be sittin' in. Best to praise this sun,
shinin' its dry shine. *Lawd have mercy, son,*

is it coming? Such a strong man, my son.
Can't help but believe when he tells us, *Wait.*
Wait some more. Wish some trees would block this sun.
We wait. Ain't no white men or buses come,
but look—see that there? Get me out this chair,
help me stand on up. No time for sleepin',

cause look what's rumbling this way. If you sleep
you gon' miss it. *Look there,* I tell my son.
He don't hear. I'm 'bout to get out this chair,
but the ghost in my legs tells me to wait,
wait for the salvation that's sho to come.
I see my savior's face 'longside that sun.

Nobody sees me running toward the sun.
Lawd, they think I done gone and fell asleep.
They don't hear *Come.*

Come.
Come.
Come.
Come.
Come.
Come.
Ain't but one power make me leave my son.
I can't wait, Herbert. Lawd knows I can't wait.
Don't cry, boy, I ain't in that chair no more.

Wish you coulda come on this journey, son,
seen that ol' sweet sun lift me out of sleep.
Didn't have to wait. And see my golden chair?

DIDN'T NEED NO MUSIC, NEITHER

Again, for Mama Freeman

You told me they was gon' come, Herbert,
and they did, dressed in the kind of white that blinds,
and they whole body was hands, moving grace
over dust, pulling circle straight. Every bone
all of a sudden like that music a blind man makes
when he leaning on just one organ key.
You tole me *Wait, mama, they almost here.*
And they came quiet,
roundabout and back door like breeze,
then they said

Ethel

Mayo

Freeman

just as clear and plain.
You didn't see them, boy, you ain't seen me walk away
with one of them on each arm like a li'l ol' sassy gal?
Don't tell me you missed mama on her ol' legs
dancing with them pretty mens in the mud?

THANKFUL

"What I'm hearing is they all want to stay in Texas. Everyone is so overwhelmed by the hospitality . . . And so many of the people in the arena here, you know, were underprivileged anyway, so this—this [chuckles slightly] is working very well for them."
—BARBARA BUSH, TOURING A HURRICANE RELIEF CENTER IN HOUSTON

Our mothers once crafted banquets
from chicken necks, or that part of a hog's belly,
whatever it was, that dragged low in its shit.
They decorated mirrored shadowboxes
with chipped porcelain nothing-at-alls,
jelly glasses, or white dolls stunned in their gingham.
They tossed threadbare throws over sunken divans
quickly flicking the slower roaches away
and insisting that you *sit down, sit down.*
Offering up a smudged glass of faucet water
or grape Kool-Aid stiff with blanched sugar,
they went on and on about mustard vs. collards,
church hats, press curls, insurance books and,
of course, Reverend Adam's stuck-up new lady friend.
Hearing squeals, they rushed to dust-crusted windows
and saw brick kissing brick, watched us poppin'
our little hips to hot rhymes, grinding thin knees
into glass and concrete, bleeding with play.
Stop playin' with them boys, girl, and put that sweater on!

God only knew where their men were.
Rumor had it they were sucked into factories
and so hollowed by whistle time
that even a woman's blue crave,
even the promise of some marbled meat
drowned in pepper sauce and sliced turnip,
couldn't lure them back home.

Our mamas daily squawked hallelujahs
toward scarred walls, conjured stout suppers
of sweet fried bread and fat, longed for missing men,
cursed crafty rodents snickering duets behind the stove.
What fools they were to think it golden.
Thank you for the ice eye, the impish giggle,
for reminding all our mothers to be damned.

34

ST. BERNARD PARISH, LA., Sept. 7 (UPI)—Thirty-four bodies were found drowned in a nursing home where people did not evacuate. More than half of the residents of St. Rita's Nursing Home, 20 miles southeast from downtown New Orleans, died August 29 when floodwaters from Hurricane Katrina reached the home's roof.

1.

I believe Jesus is hugely who He says He is:
The crook of an arm,
a shadow threatening my hair.
a hellish glare beneath the moonwash,
the slapping storm that wakes me,
the washing clean.

2.

The Reaper has touched his lips to my days,
blessing me with gray fragrance and awkward new skin.
What makes the dust of me smell like a dashed miracle,
the underside of everything?
What requires me to hear the bones?

3.

Before the rain stung like silver, I had forgotten me.
My name was a rude visitor, arriving
unannounced, without a gift,
always leaving too soon.

4.
If you knew my alley, its stink and blue,
if you knew dirt-gritted collard greens
salt-pork slick and doused with Tabasco,
then you knew me.
I know that you've come
with my engine, and the rest of my skin.
You will rise me.

5.
Son don't rise,
daughter don't know enough to dial a phone.
Gets harder to remember
how my womb folded because of them,
how all of me lumbered with their foolish weight.
See what they have done,
how hard and sweet they done dropped me here?

6.
Clumps of earth in the rising and me
too weathered to birth a howl.
I sleep in small shatters. I climb
the bitten left wall of my heart.
In all the places I fall,
it is dry.

7.
We knew we had been bred for sacrifice,
our overflow of yesterdays too wretched a nudge,
our tired hearts borderless
and already mapped for the Motherland.
We reach for the past like it is food and we are starving.
Our surfaces are scoured.

We are prepared.
We are wrapped in white.

8.
When help comes,
it will be young men smelling like cigarettes and Chevys,
muscled boys with autumn breath and steel baskets
just the right size for our souls.
To save us, they will rub our gums with hard bread.
They will offer us
water.

9.
To cool fever, rub the sickness with wet earth.
For swelling, boil a just-plucked chicken
and douse the hurt in the steam.
Always from the position of the knees,
create the savior you need.
Then
wait.

Wait.

Jesus . . . both faith and magic have failed.

10.
There is no light, no thin food moving through my arms.
Even without machines, I feel my numbers have soared.
I am a sudden second of soft leaving.
I'm cold
and I'm strapped to this country.

11.
Daughter, son, I am bursting with this.
I am straining to celebrate the links of blood.
I am wide aloud craving something shaped like you.

12.
There are no bridges.

13.
We are stunned on our scabbed backs.
There is the sound of whispered splashing,
and then this:

Leave them.

14.
Our father
which art in heaven . . .

15.
The walls are slithering with Bayou spit,
tears,
the badness that muddies rivers.
We flail in that sin,
alive and bended beneath a wretched Southern rain.
We sip our breath from that filthy ocean.
Only some things float.

16.
I ain't scared of no wet, no wave. I done seen more than this.
God is in *all* houses.
Just balance the huge noun of Him on your tongue.

17.
Wait with me.
Watch me sleep in this room
that looks so much like night.
I'm gon' wake up, I swear it,
to some kind of sun.

18.

19.
My name Earline
and I'm gon' say you my life—
sugar in my veins, a single cloudy eye,
and blood when I pee.
Half dead, I used to say,
I used to tell 'em *Hell, I'm already half dead.*

20.
I have forgotten how to pray,
cannot find my knees.

I want the man with my needles.
I want that sting,
those silver holes in my body, I want
my needles,
I want my sleep for days,
I wanna cheat the Reaper.

I want somebody's hand.

21.
Hallowed be thy name

22.
Hollow be *our* names.
Call us running boards, the ice man,
big band, hogshead, possum in stewing pots.
Twist our heads on our snapping necks
back to where we danced from.
Call us names that are barely necessary.
Call us those
who do not need these days.

23.
Big Easy.
I ran your green,
rolled in your red dust,
and your sun turned the white of me red
and the black of me blue.
Funny how colored I got,
how I absorbed your heat, and how you,
without flinching,
called me your child.

24.
God, we need your glitter, you know,
those wacky miracles
you do
for no reason at all?

25.
I fight the rise with all the guitar left in my throat.
Old folks got shit to say,
ain't got but a little time to say it.
We don't never die quiet.

26.
A sudden ocean of everyone's shoulders.

27.
And this scripture: *Leave them.*

28.
And I am left, no deity hovering,
no black hair on my head,
all of me thinner than when I began.

Fingers of ice climb me,
reach my dimming light,
and choke my only angel.

29.
I had the rumble hips, I tell ya.
I was sling-back and press curl
and big titties with necessary milk.
I was somebody's woman,
I was the city where the city wasn't.
Louisiana,
goddamn.
You lied to me so lush.

30.
I lost my seeing in that war.
But I ain't gonna need these old eyes for that resurrection.

That's gon' be one *hell* of a line.

I'll be the one slightly off center.
I might be facing the wrong way.

31.
They left us. Me. Him. Our crinkled hands.
They left our hard histories, our gone children and storytells.
They left the porch creaking.
They left us to our God,
but our God was mesmerized elsewhere,
watching His rain.

32.
Thy will be done.

33.
No more of us,
stunned and silent on the skin of this sea,
this thunderous wet.
We bob and bounce and spin slow,
draped in an odd sparkle.

34.
The underearth turns its face to us.

leave

    them

THEIR SAVIOR WAS ME

Now, everything that breathes
knows my given name, the full of it,
the scars it leaves on the skyline.
They know my moments of mercy,
and yes, how calmly I can kill.
The bastard child of a bluesman and an ocean,
I won't die until music does. But I

have never heard a prayer
that began with my name,
gave me pause,
forced me to rearrange my wind.
Instead, I listened, bemused, to thirty-four
snotty pleas addressed to the idea of *Him,*
the ghost in the air, my rumored father.

I was all the seconds they had left.
They should have smothered me with kneeling.
Instead, in their old scratched voices,
they begged the wet air for salvation. They called
Lord, Lord, Lord,
until I was forced to show them my face.

VOODOO VI: HEALING

Lay curlicued words directly upon the death,
silk side down. Grind wildflowers until they
have misted and become much closer to air,
then rub the bursted smell into the harm.
Separate God's name from your prayer, and hope
He remembers the brutal long-ago ways of magick:
Blood in the water.
Blood cleanses the water.

LOOKING FOR BODIES

I.

Slowly push the door open with your foot
because wood that has been wet for so long
gives to touch, imitates flesh.
Do not kick the door open,
no matter how weirdly your heart drums.
There may be something all wrong behind it.
Push and immediately drown
in what could be ordinary, if ordinary was
a crusted saucepan, toppled rockers,
pine-framed portraits of newly
baptized babies and fathers with an overload of teeth.
Allow yourself his lunatic smile as you spy
signs of ritual and days undone—
bright ghosts of skirts and workshirts,
or the spiraled grace of decapitated dolls
doing their blind dance, bumping your knees.

Eventually you will need these diversions.
You will lock your fractured heart upon them,
because what you will see next
will hurt you long and aloud.
A monstered smell sings her out of hiding,
and at first you believe
that one doll, plumper than the rest

and still intact,
survived the deluge,
but then you—

II.

guide the gold of her into
your arms blessing the droop
and blown skin marveling
at the way her soul rides
slickly on the outside of
everything how it ripples
the water how it so deftly
damns your hands

VOODOO VII:
DEVELOP PSYCHIC POWERS

which will allow you to whisper the next visit,
to pack up your picture frames and pills,
to point your battered car toward the mouth
of the interstate. To *go*, ashed and angry,
into more south, softer rain. You can shake doors,
pull your neighbors up by their thick roots.
You can scurry the streets,
wild waving your jazz hands,
screaming the changed dawn.
This time, you can nail shut the windows,
wrap your world in clouded plastic,
watch her thick torso disturb the cloud line.
Feeling her spit before it touches you,
you'll fold your body against her breath
before it pushes you forward, roughly,
surrendering your chicken ass to a future
of skirting drama, and dying somewhere else.

BURIED

"We do not dig graves or put caskets into graves any longer. The decision was made and funeral homes were notified that families and funeral homes would have to supply grave-digging personnel."
—ED MAZOUE, NEW ORLEANS CITY REAL ESTATE ADMINISTRATOR AND PERSON IN CHARGE OF THE CITY'S CEMETERIES

There's nothing but mud. The ground looks dry and firm,
but underneath is a stew of storm. Stout shovels, rusted,
grow gummed and heavy with what I heft and rearrange.

Progress is slow.

The sun so often steams me shut, and I have to stop
to gulp sugared bites of tea,
flick away sweat with my swollen fingers,
swat hard at sluggish flies who hover,

like they know.

And when I start again, there's a rhythm to it,
some ticking jazz that gets my square hips involved.
I craft a chant purely for downbeat:
Plunge. Push. Lift. Toss it.
Plunge. Push. Lift. Toss it.
My untried muscles blaze,
joints click,
pulse clutches my chest.

Whole clocks later, I pause to relish the feat,
to marvel at the way I've compromised the earth,
how I've been that kind of God for a minute.
But only time has moved.
It's like trying to reach the next world with a spoon.

My boy would have laughed.
Daddy, you better sit down and watch some ball game,
and we'd settle, Sunday lazy,
his squirm balanced on my belly.

He needed what I was and what I wasn't.
Giggling in little language, he lobbed me the ball soft,
walked slower when I was at his side,
shared puffed white bread and purple jelly.
He waited patiently for me after dark
while I shuffled piles of books, looking for
a bedtime drama of spacemen or soldiers,
some crayoned splash to wrap his day around.

But every night, when I opened the door to his room,
all I saw
was a quivering mountain of Snoopys, Blues, and Scoobys.
Underneath them, his happy body could barely cage breath.
Giggles unleashed his toes. My line, then: *Where are yoooou?*

Plunge. Push. Lift. Toss it.

Plunge. Push. Lift. Toss—

With the dirt balanced high, screaming my shoulder,
I think hard on those nights of tussle and squeal.
I want to feel his heat and twist in my arms again.

I have to dig.

BACK HOME

Everything crawls—the green-black walls
move slow like prayer. The floor rocks
with all that's left living—leggy
scuttering, vermin, lumpy rain.
Everything floats dizzy samba,
weaving obstacles and channels,
and sometimes rats ride. This is home.
This is home as funk, churning moss
dripping from its arms, arms open
wide to take in my damp body.
Everything crawls. The drooped ceiling
crawls toward the floor, the light hard-crawls
through soft splintered slats. And I crawl
through upturned rooms, humming gospel,
closing tired eyes against my home's
languid rhythms of rot, begging
my new history to hold still.

REMEMBERING TO SING

torch
spices
till the smoke bites
your walls

string glass beads
onto red thread
then drape

from the neckbone
of a priestess

drink only wine
that is thick with lying
to you. try to

sleep

sing every word
of whatever you don't dream

sing every
word

WHAT BETSY HAS TO SAY

In 1965, Hurricane Betsy swept through the Bahamas and South Florida, then hit the Louisiana coast, flooding New Orleans. During the four days of the storm, 75 people died.

No nuance. Got no whisper
in you, do you girl?

The idea was not
to stomp it flat, 'trina,
all you had to do was *kiss* the land,
brush your thunderous lips against it
and leave it stuttering, scared barren
at your very notion. Instead,

you roared through like
a goddamned man, all biceps and must,
flinging your dreaded mane
and lifting souls up to feed your ravenous eye.

I thought I taught you better, girl.
I showed you the right way to romance that city,
how to break its heart
and leave it pining for more of your slap.

So if this was your way of erasing me,
turning me from rough lesson to raindrop,
you did it ugly, chile. Yeah, I truly enjoyed

being God for that minute. But unlike you,
rash gal, I left some of my signature standing.
I only killed what got in my way.

LUTHER B ASCENDS

sketched against a wearied patch
of earth,

smashed level with the mud,
smalled

by roaring days, and a sky
he trusted,

this beast
this child

REBUILDING

A razored sky, unsure of what it yields,
arcs over flattened blocks, upturned faces,
muted shards of organ. Each day reveals
inane thoughts of dance. All fleeting traces
of the needled rain, the roar, the black wind
swirl in the obscene shimmer of new nails
hammered into treated wood. The thick-skinned
bring a song up from their feet, but it fails
to drown out the big useless drone of work,
the busy sounds of lifting what is damned.
Paint the rubble pretty, hues gone berserk
with dry hope. It seems we have been programmed
to set chaos upright, scrub at the stain,
build our homes on rivers, waltz in the rain.

GOLDEN RULE DAYS

Following Katrina, thousands of schoolchildren were forced to work through trauma while they adjusted to new schools, cultures, and communities. Their reception has ranged from pity, to acceptance, to blatant exclusion.

I.

They keep touching him. They keep touching
him, as if they expect his surface to suddenly
wilt, as if they could actually feel the water
sloshing in place of a heart. Their thousand
hands are curved and comforting, heat cupped
in them like money, arid swipes in each of their
fingers. *We're sorry, we're sorry.* They keep
touching him, brushing past his scarred arms,
tugging lightly on his clothing, some boldly
reaching out for his cheek, *sorry, so sorry.*
And he wonders how long he can stand this
still, be this sort of trophy, how long he can stay
bended, going from one to the other, slipping
their winged feet into God's loafers, slipping
deftly into his role as child who drowns, again
and again, who opens his mouth to scream,
but river rushes in. His saviors believe with all
their hearts in soft rescues. They keep touching him.

II.

Her name is A-R-L-I-N-E, an old woman's name
from a grandmama's way of spelling,
and her shoes are smeared with her home
and laced with string. Too nappy and ashed
for first day, she walks in halting,
but dippin' bayou like she's got one fluid hip
and knows some real old music real well.
she is prepared to be anyone, anything.
With just a little warning, she can juggle
language, gone days, she can recite lines
scripted to staunch questions and add light
to her skin. Replace the *i* in her name with an *e*,
yes, start there, with what she is called. Then
shield her against the murdering rain, which
just keeps drumming her dizzy, naming her over.

III.

Carla rose from the black river
and was resurrected as refugee
pickaninny
unfortunate swimmer
gasper
She woke up in the wrong country
her donated denims too snug
too not-hers
their pocked hips made her
instantly recognizable as
Katrina girl
as plaits undone
as double negative

as hard case
loud on these white streets
and so easily summoned now
by snicker, the tooth suck, that noun.

Carla rose from the black river
unraveled, rattled,
unrhymed,

> *What's the matter*

alone, unwhole, choking on gas
and rot

> *nigger*

but what a caress
beneath the water's shifting

> *couldn't you*

surface
> *swim?*

GIVE ME MY NAME

A paper tag was pinned to her T-shirt.
The blue blurring must have been her name.
She had died next to someone who wanted
her whole and known in this world.
Now her fingerprints slide away with the skin
of her fingers. Five days in the putrid water
have doubled her, slapped the brown light
from her body. She could be anyone now,
pudged, eyeless, oddly gray.

Now she's one of silver's citizens,
filed with her breathless sisters,
all of them waiting for a smidgen of spit,
a hair caught in a discarded brush,
a sliver of bone to script their stories,
rub the killing flood from their numbers.

No one removes her tag, its careful letters
now just flat blue smashes of spiral and line.
This is all the breath there is in the room.
It is the only thing not saying
give her back to the water.
It is the only thing not saying dead.

SIBLINGS

Hurricanes, 2005

Arlene learned to dance backwards in heels that were too high.
Bret prayed for a shaggy mustache made of mud and hair.
Cindy just couldn't keep her windy legs together.
Dennis never learned to swim.
Emily whispered her gusts into a thousand skins.
Franklin, farsighted and anxious, bumbled villages.
Gert spat her matronly name against a city's flat face.
Harvey hurled a wailing child high.
Irene, the baby girl, threw pounding tantrums.
José liked the whip sound of slapping.
Lee just craved the whip.
Maria's thunder skirts flew high when she danced.
Nate was mannered and practical. He stormed precisely.
Ophelia nibbled weirdly on the tips of depressions.
Philippe slept too late, flailing on a wronged ocean.
Rita was a vicious flirt. She woke Philippe with rumors.
Stan was born business, a gobbler of steel.
Tammy crooned country, getting the words all wrong.
Vince died before anyone could remember his name.
Wilma opened her maw wide, flashing rot.

None of them talked about Katrina.
She was their odd sister,
the blood dazzler.

KATRINA

Weather is nothing until it reaches skin,
freezes dust, spits its little swords.
Kept to oceans, feeding only on salted water,
I was a rudderless woman in full tantrum,
throwing my body against worlds I wanted.
I never saw harm in lending that ache.
All I ever wanted to be
was a wet, gorgeous mistake,
a reason to crave shelter.

VOODOO VIII:
SPIRITUAL CLEANSING & BLESSING

There's no deception like the world after rain.
Suddenly God is everywhere,
winking from dumpster rivers,
using the insistent perfume of plain water
to scrape funk from alleyways and men.
In the seconds after storm,
we sign on for brash little resurrections.
We lose those ten pesky pounds,
resolve to enthusiastically fuck dim spouses,
stop reaching across breakfast tables
to slap our children into silence.
We straighten framed blacklight squares
of The Last Supper, musing upon the wide
sad eyes of wept clarity and looming doom.
And we are comforted until the sun
blazes the stench forward, rebirthing rot
and workdays. Then His eyes are dry,
threaded with lightning and hurt,
and we are reminded, again,
just what He's capable of.

COLOPHON

Blood Dazzler was designed at Coffee House Press,
in the historic warehouse district of downtown Minneapolis.
Fonts include Caslon and Scala Sans.

FUNDER ACKNOWLEDGMENTS

Coffee House Press is an independent nonprofit literary publisher. Our books are made possible through the generous support of grants and gifts from many foundations, corporate giving programs, state and federal support, and through donations from individuals who believe in the transformational power of literature. Coffee House Press receives general operating support from the Minnesota State Arts Board, through an appropriation by the Minnesota State Legislature and from the National Endowment for the Arts, and major general operating support from the McKnight Foundation, and from Target. Coffee House also receives support from: two anonymous donors; the Elmer L. and Eleanor J. Andersen Foundation; Bill Berkson; the Buuck Family Foundation; the Patrick and Aimee Butler Family Foundation; Jennifer Haugh; Joanne Hilton; Stephen and Isabel Keating; the Kenneth Koch Literary Estate; Allan and Cinda Kornblum; Seymour Kornblum and Gerry Lauter; Kathryn and Dean Koutsky; Ethan J. Litman; Mary McDermid; Stu Wilson and Melissa Barker; the Lenfestey Family Foundation; Rebecca Rand; the law firm of Schwegman, Lundberg, Woessner, PA.; Charles Steffey and Suzannah Martin; the James R. Thorpe Foundation; the Woessner Freeman Family Foundation; the Wood-Rill Foundation; and many other generous individual donors.

This activity is made possible in part by a grant from the Minnesota State Arts Board, through an appropriation by the Minnesota State Legislature and a grant from the National Endowment for the Arts. MINNESOTA STATE ARTS BOARD   **TARGET**

To you and our many readers across the country,
we send our thanks for your continuing support.

Good books are brewing at coffeehousepress.org